Bodies Not Our Own

Books by William Page

Bodies Not Our Own (1986)
The Gatekeeper (1982)
Clutch Plates (1976)

Bodies Not Our Own

Poems by

William Page

MEMPHIS STATE UNIVERSITY PRESS

Grateful acknowledgement is made to the following magazines in which most of the poems in this collection first appeared, some in earlier forms: *The Chariton Review, Cottonwood Review, DeKalb Literary Arts Journal, Eleven, Eureka, The Louisville Review, Mississippi Review, The National Forum, The North American Review, Ploughshares, Poem, Porch, The Southern Review, Southwest Review, Webster Review, Wind Literary Journal, The Windless Orchard.* "Devotion," "The Girl in the Iron Lung," and "Saying It All" first appeared in the *Cimarron Review* and are reprinted here with the permission of the Board of Regents for Oklahoma State University, holders of the copyright. "Learning the Basics" first appeared in *Kansas Quarterly.* "For One Who Has No Heart" first appeared in *Three Rivers Poetry Journal*, copyright © 1982 by Three Rivers Press.

Manufactured in the United States of America
ISBN 0–87870–210–5
Library of Congress Cataloging in Publication Data

Page, William, 1929–
    Bodies not our own.

    I. Title.
PS3566.A337B6   1986   811'.54   85-31049
ISBN 0-87870-210-5

For my son, Vince

My special thanks to the Walter R. Smith Distinguished Book Award Committee for bestowing the 1985 award upon this book. Also my thanks to Jay Meek for his comments on my original manuscript and to others, especially my wife, Nancy, for their support and encouragement.

Contents

Dust

Dust

To these slate painted windows
I come back where I learned,
to these smells of wet cement and urine,
the bricks and glass of public schools.
I return for the lost sake of those who taught,
for the long division of now and then,
and for the swing hung in the sun
while a child ran under, shouting
the now forgotten name. I come
to leave the cotton from these knickers,
to call back the names of faithful teaching
matrons, of skinny spinsters, and widows—all
who gave me their brothers lost in the Argonne,
who told the story of the Hindenburg aflame,
and explained how the many small numbers
could be made into the large one.
I render unto Caesar and the seasons
or whoever will listen: the Mississippi,
the Nile, and the Aegean.
I recite the capitals of the states
and spell the seaports of the world.
Then this paltry list of facts
I buckle up with my strap
and leave it for what it was.
I hold between my fingers
these once millions of tiny creatures
who memorialized *their* teacher
the buxom sea by dying into chalk.
I write in bold white letters
my own three names and each teacher's
erotic title I can remember,
and the rest I consign to dust.

What We Did Before Sex

Little girls could not understand
the pungent charm, the sticky mystique
of airplane glue. In those days
we knew to open the windows wide.
To keep our eyes clear, the vision
pure. It was the magic of stillness
a boy had to learn, if the wing
was to grow firm as it had to.
The waiting was all the hardest.
The pulling off of our finger tips,
the stripping of scales from our hands
never left us as freaks. The translucent
scabs took cells we never missed.
Of the whole operation, using
the double blade, sharp as the
twin edges of daring and fear,
taught us to cut through our need
precisely and true, though there were
slips we paid for with blood,
with the red sting of iodine,
and the rage of ruined wings.
We used a wood light and porous
and feared most the rubber's snap.
The best of motors were just short
of one too many winds. The skin
of our machines was common
though delicately thin, usually
red or green, the symbols
that made us stop, then let us go
passing as we did through childhood.

Devotion

I step out of your big car
touching its hood like a coffin,
putting one small foot
across the ditch.
You hold the gun
its two barrels morning
and night. Brown water
stands in the ditch.
It is an undistinguished field
where ceremonial birds
are not going to fly
though we are dressed
for the first kill.
They have scattered,
disciples of the twelve winds,
and will not return
to this livid sky.
I am here not like
the two spotted retrievers,
for they have seen
such fields, and such skies
alive with small flesh.
And you let them out
to run gloriously,
mad with the scent they carry,
a quivering in each nostril.
The wild animal is me,
the one hungry for hunt.
Your jacket is heavy
with icons: pellets and powder,
blood and grass
and the dyed cylinders

capped with brass circles
on each stamped
a shape of eternity.
The bags we have brought
each for four birds
are folded temples
and hang from a canvas strap
looped on your holy shoulders,
though it is not a question of sainthood,
but of suffering a son's devotion.

The Heavens

for Aunt Pinkie

As this fried egg sizzles
up in the pan, I can smell
the one *you* cooked so long ago.
And since I know even
the sulphurous sun lasts only
so long, that the sunflowers
that bloomed in your garden
turned dark and are gone

and since this morning
is as good as any other,
I remember your name:
your favorite color
that hangs like a sweater
in the closet of my dreams.

Back in your kitchen,
in nineteen thirty-nine,
you crinkled a sack
into a sound of fire
and felt my cheeks until you said
they tingled from the kisses of un-
seen fairies who'd gone
to live inside the stars.

You laughed and dropped
our finished dishes into the foam,
while I looked in the yard
to the pool to see a single fin
shining near the surface.

And as night came flowing
from the edges of moon
I watched the heavens,
and exactly as you'd said
I saw them light up the sky
with their tiny rooms.

This morning, I watch
the clouds pinken into day,
and a light comes back
as if from you.

Coppers

He kept them in a tin box
on the mantle and called
them coppers. By then
the moon was damp
in his old eyes, and the sun
hung like a fob,
a time when the nights
grew in the orchard
with the ripe plums.
There's always a smell
of white linen gone to yellow
when the old come to look out
the window to see the frog
that could never be a prince
hop up the road and around
the bend never to return.
Many an old grandfather wore
suspenders and spat
in a can. One I knew
stood looking at a field
where each stalk of burley
reminded him of a son.
I knew this one who changed
his name on his death bed.
Trouble, my grandfather used
to say, leaves of its own accord;
one man drives twenty miles
to a sulphur spring, another
pumps for years trying to get
his clear. Boy, these coppers
I save in the box I give to you
not because they are shiny and round

but because I love you and wish
you to know what each child
can understand: that a thing
ungiven is nothing.

The Salvation of Uncle Floyd

Uncle Floyd's head comes bobbing up,
the cigar still smoking, words
seeping like cheap wine
from the corners of his mouth.
He strikes a match in my skull,
peering across the forgotten years.
There's the office he clerked
in, there's the bar tended
the year he was on the wagon.
Tattooed on his forearm, a drunk
sprawls in a slumway door. He
recognizes it; it's him.
Uncle Floyd blinks hard, until his eyes
clear. His mind's like a journal
entry glistening. He takes
the Havana from his mouth
and pronounces his name—Master
Sergeant Floyd Coile, born again in
the U.S. Army, his pocket full
of pencils. The typing ribbon
and the multicolored forms
have saved him. He signs
himself the man of letters,
the clerk, the right hand
of printed orders, the promoter,
the demoter, potato peeling
detail, sick call, leaves, and
A.W.O.L.'s. Uncle Floyd, ready for
the reenlistment binge.

Not a Word

She heard the rain
ringing in the well,
the salt of the smoke house
singing. She hummed
past the swinging hams,
the nests full of eggs
shining like moons.

Halos spun on her apron;
mules sweated in the fields.
She raised her hand
to hold a claw, a knife
which never frowned.

Peeling apples that curled
in snakes,
she smelled of dough
and shadows of swallows
high in the barn.

She threw the grain
in a circle of chickens,
the tractor rusting,
the plow saying not a word,
the tall barn saying
not a word to warn her.

Phosphate

With hills
banked up against the sky
horizons steamed
up to meet the sun
that melted down
each day
along the ridge
where trees burned,
then ashened into shade.

While downhill
trucks left behind
turbulent smoke,
and in the dust
that settled on the ground
we traced our names
and looked for God or fun.
And wondered as we played:

Why the town drunk lay down
with a smoldering cigarette
and burned to glory
in a hotel room
or why his drinking buddy
flamed with real religion
and why the pitted fields
ran down to crimson rivers.

One boy remembered
the blazing green of the hummingbird
hovering above forsythia,
another the gray front steps

where he handed his mother
a rose under a scarlet sun
or where he fell on the glazed ice
that shone like fire
and broke his pitching arm.

Once a week people met
in the town square, always
on Saturday, the day to shop
and swear how hot, or cold, it was,
to look upon the splattered soldier
facing North and talk about
the fumes that fell upon
the fields and killed the crops.

Going Around

Again and again the small plane circles
in the sky that never ends.
My brother yelled contact
and swung on the prop
while Dad said, "Switch on: Begin."
I pulled up the door
that shut us in.
We took off
from a dusty field,
and looking back I tried
to see the straight tracks
left by the two small wheels.
Below us the windsock
had a hard on, surrounded
by fence rows and fields.
The wooden prop chattered
like an angry aunt
against the buffeting wind.
The cylinders' heat
was all we needed
to keep us warm.
We stalled at the sun
and dived with a delighted squeal.

*

The lace napkins my mother says
she'll leave to her daughters-in-law,
the silver to my oldest sister.
On the handles are designs
like revolving propellers.
And now as I look at the past

through a plastic windshield
I hear the droning motor
humming on and on and on.

Spring Forward, Fall Back

It began when the scissors
were straight up on the clock
while the big breast of moon
was feeding her stars.
I was a child sleeping in the springs
of my body, at a time when we listened
for victory to chime up the spires
in each separate but hopeful garden.
Then Mother pushed the hand
around in a circle.

Months went by and the seasons
turned like gears into autumn
while twice a day the clock
raised up its arms.
But in the fall as the sun
prepared one night to sleep
the extra hour, Father forgot
when the hands overlapped.

We arose, and thinking
we washed the usual night
from our faces, we set out
in the early shadows
to soil our hands or hearts.
At school I drifted from the car
as it melted away and sat down
alone in the dim hour of doom
in a child's vision of fear
until it burst with the sound
of a yellow sun topping the hill
with a bus full of children

and my heart rang like a bell
as I knew the world
had not yet run down.

Aim

I stood on a porch,
the balance of my air rifle braced
against a post, and took aim
through the metal yoke
seeing the green and yellow finch
they called gold. The sky didn't
rumble to warn me, or the bird.
But I tripped and the bird hurled
into space, saving us both.
The same day, closing the cup of a hollyhock
in a single instant, I took a bee,
its legs pressed against
the stamen. No humming of choirs
could halt me. When autumn came
I carried the leaves in a bundle
like a hunchback in a story,
then struck them into fire,
scorching the curb black,
shadowing the world with my dark cloud.
Finally I grew, I learned to lie
and throw the shadow
of a man, took a job laying brick
and slaved for thirty years,
bought a house and taught
three kids how hard life could be
if you keep yourself alarmed.
Now the kids have moved away,
the wife sits with TV, the cat
and dog stand waiting
to be fed. Sometimes,
I ask what went flying

off those years ago
when I thought it was a bird.

To Begin

In Memoriam:
Columbia Military Academy
1905–1978

The itch of blue sky
covers me like wool.
If I look quickly
I'll see the thin shadows
running from themselves,
the battalions of light
blowing away with the years.
The bugle boy with one eye
winks as if to say,
"Forgive."

       The flag
unfurls atop the brass mast,
upside down the whole year.
Somewhere an oily bolt
is clicking, rows
of black shoes shine
like the balls of a cannon.
A saber is drawn from its sheath.

       Even as I wave
the cape of my tongue,
a voice floating in milk
gives commands in a language
no one can follow. And in the next
room everyone who stood at attention
is leaving. In a moment
I will turn over in bed

waiting for the orders
of this day to begin.

Static

The Scholar Who Loved Plath

Everyone would remember this day
better than he; the morning
would fall from the sky
as if nothing mattered as usual.
He would make up his bed,
folding the corners like a finished book.

For breakfast nothing would do.
By ten o'clock the air would be calling
to say noon would sag, a sinking balloon.

He climbs the stairs, passing
the seven floorless rooms.
He carries two black volumes
one for life and one for death,
opens the mirror of now and then

and steps in to surprise himself,
leaving below only a darkening ring,
the circle left by his coffee cup.

Lost Change

The Old Man of Moving Pictures,
you slipped past the usher
and the broken sweeper
where time lies on the floor
like sweetened gum.
We're swallowed back,
husks of cold popcorn.
The footlights shine, and fake
velvet chairs clap their seats.
Old films reel from the tall balcony.
Making perfect circles, light flashing
from your hand, you float down the aisle.
And a chill drifts down like tickets.
You brought us through doors
under the blazing marquee.
You dimmed the lights
and opened the curtains
on the bright, flat scenes.
But now, you're with the vast dark house
where the last reel's ended
and light's sucked back
from the great blank screen.

From What I Remember

And now the room
is forever dark,
someone else is sleeping,
or a light flashes on
and the bacon begins to blister.
Last night I called another state
and discovered a whole town
is missing from what I remember.

*

I can imagine the imprint
of your left hip on a right
front fender, in bright daylight
while someone was buying
a birthday card in Toledo
to send God knows where.
You smoked your last cigarette,
taught your last lesson
and set out on your daily walk.
That much I'm sure of.
Well, strange as it may
seem, I must say
it cured you of walking
in the streets, it solved
your problem of looking
for a mate. We all died
in an Ohio blizzard, frozen
into ourselves little by little.
But this of course is different,
and forces me to talk nonsense.
I wish there could be

one big book with all
our friends' numbers.
I could call them all
and tell each one: how you must
have crawled off in the weeds
while the brown car sped on.
Perhaps you were wearing
your thick glasses that
shattered into slivers
or the contacts simply popped
past your startled lids,
as you had a vision
of the snow angel some kid
had made for you last winter.

Static

I watched them saw through the ribs
and take from his sack of membranes
a man's beating heart. And he lived.

But late tonight, only gray rain
pours from this hissing screen

while outside thunder sounds
like a starter's gun

and somewhere, fogs away,
a runner lies in his lost race.

Though I wished for him a sunny win,
with each fantastic stride

the spongy soles rising higher,
his lungs filled with light,

I know instead he sleeps into each
slow step, till none is left.

And I move across my measured room
against the jogging glow

and pressing the switch
I let it go

as the racing universe
will let me go, dashing back
into the swirling static.

Prediction

You fed the cats in the roots of trees,
poured pitchers of milk in hollow stumps.

Each day you've said you seemed to kiss again
the dusty face of an old mongrel

as when you wore no shoes and held in each hand
a dainty swatch of Queen Anne's lace.

It drifts through time like moist
flakes that touched the nose on cold days.

Last week you said you saw a doll's eyes open
as you glanced in the toy shop window.

Yesterday your vocabulary seemed to shrink,
your vowels sounded strangely high.

And tonight in the midst of such quiet breathing,
I reach across the bed and feel you're gone.

The Grave Digger's Son

Learning the Basics

I crossed through the gates
entering hell, thinking
what have I done this day,
leaving the winding rivers
in the streets behind me,
leaving the small bridges
that crossed into the heavenly city
I would be forbidden to see.
It would be weeks before
I saw anyone not naked
or wearing a uniform,
months before anyone called me
by a Christian name.
And all the while the river
that never forgot
flowed through the saintly city
carrying the eyes we'd cast in.
Here would be those
I would remember even after
they forgot themselves,
the sergeant riding backwards
on his cycle, the stupid cook
who couldn't smell.
And when we ran free for half a day
fear saved some from the jagged
tattoos, from women
who offered what we wanted
but could not pay.
In the compound
our lives formed at dawn
when we left the beds
still thick with sleep.

The waking days were spent
in marching, the nights
we memorized the sun.
And when time came to leave
the camp of the living dead,
we entered life once more
thinking we were men
who could never again be killed.

After the War

Shivering in back of a truck,
huddled over a bundle of all I own

I'm clapping my hands, not for the
driver's attention, nor for the pleasure

of heading home, but only to keep
them warm. On this lurching truck

that allows no sleep, above two
tracks that trail in snow

on the hidden road of the cold horizon,
the sun is slowly rising.

In a matter of miles
in warmer hours

I'm hitching by car
through the viscous rain.

Closer to the home I haven't seen
for years, I come
carrying new hope in an old wound.

Learning To Take It

Father parks his car and goes in
through the basement door.
He crosses the concrete floor,
and setting his foot on the first stair
he passes the iron furnace,
remembers the cold winter
he'd filled it with coal
as the fire made him sweat
and he emptied each shovel with a groan.
But now it's spring and the windows
upstairs are open for all
the neighbors to hear his silence
as he makes his way to the dining table.
Mother complains of everything,
beginning with the sloppy job
he did of sweeping the walk,
with a worn-out broom, and ends
recounting the brown stain on a napkin
made many years ago by one of his friends.
All the while Father's said nothing,
except pass the Spam.
At the end of the meal
he rises from the table,
coughs, puts on his glasses.
And without a word, moves
through the living room
on to the porch to read the papers,
which in spite of their words
remain silent forever.

The Face

I don't remember the first sunset
rounding the flat prairie
nor the last word before the last.
But I do recall the dog's running
toward the slowing traffic
and the bouncing sound it made
before it turned, limping back
to where it started from
as I saw it was blind.

If I were this minute to run
with my waving hair
I'd go straight for the other side,
and wouldn't I be amazed
by the sheer blinding blow
as I hit the impenetrable wall
of habit? And for all my trouble,
for all the insistent desire
to change, I'd be thrown back
as if hit by a car and limp back
into the dusty flowers with the sun
burning, arrogant like the face
of an angry father.

Valentine

The sparse black hairs
coiled under her silk pants
where I never saw them.
That summer I smelled
the wild husk burning.
But she saw the boy
who held the sponge
of a world in his hands
and squeezed it.
I looked at them and saw
her blemishes and thought
even they were beautiful
like a fashionable rouge.
I remember she danced
with a corsage pinned
near the top of her gown
where the curves of her breasts
were carefully exposed.
Above the long gloves
her scented arms
were faintly powdered.
I waited on the stairs
then passed touching faintly
against her, never dreaming
I'd be sitting here
thousands of miles away
fat and balding, still reciting
a valentine of pubic hair.

The Sickness

A cold wind blows across Lake Erie,
and Toledo has lost its leaves
a month too soon.

*

I know the minerals and acids
are the true colors in the leaves,
that the beaver works heaviest at night,
and the monarch flies two thousand miles
to a mountain it has never seen.
And that somehow it must all be right.

*

Last night I tried to sweat out
the grief of my loneliness,
but I awoke to a blizzard and the short
day of light, where months before
a field of gladiolas had bloomed.

*

As I dress in the wrinkles of my body
in the room where I wake, I see
the plants in the five pots bowed
to a sun they can only remember.
And I think again of the deer
gathered by the pond drinking
in the moon's perfect reflection.

Speaking of the Past

Last night I laid out my clothes
shoes and all, placed on
the couch just so
with the coat arms folded.
At the head and foot
I lighted a candle
of pure beeswax and sat
down trying to explain.
It was surpassing morbid
my lover said. She said
I'd lost my will.
I'm telling this
as if it were true, as if
it were only a dream
or you gave a damn.
I shook my head
as I sat there viewing,
when it came to me.
I'd laid out something
that never dies, no matter
what the ritual.

The Baton Twirlers

Soon we will sit in little rooms
and watch ourselves on a screen.
Strange anyone should think our job
is simple, is easy.
The sequence unfolds as we
watch our arms and legs
make movements impossible
to any but the faithful
who rise each morning
before the dawn and put down
the silver wand only with the last
swirl of sun. The white polish
of our boots shines like our
even teeth and is every bit
as important in the quick
routine as making our grace
appear natural and easy
like the shimmering shadows
of leaves. But skill is not the reason
we would win the viewer's love,
nor beauty luxurious with the smell
of sex. There's more to admire
in any art than tossing sticks.
Somewhere inside these nimble
pirouettes and high-kneed steps
there's untold significance
that like all religious gestures
must finally be taken on faith
even if it shows nothing of itself.

The Girl in the Iron Lung

Like you I see the same
sad face in the mirror
each day. But I
can't complain.
Yes, I'm the girl
in the iron lung,
the only child struck
in ten counties
the year sugar melted
on slick, pink tongues.
The world is divided into the
experienced and the inexperienced,
the body dragging the spirit
or; well you get the picture.
This is the same face
I also see smiling in my mirror.
I don't feel pain. I have no need
for your insistent pity.
In this tub of metal
I wear out humming motors.
One by one they fail
and I who can't even breathe,
who feel a slight pressure
on the neck can touch myself
when I please and no one sees
or even thinks of it.
And when I come alive
and moan with pleasure
and feel the wholeness of myself,
then I open my eyes
and look in the mirror

and see the lonely
face that lovers share.

The Grave Digger's Son

This is dirty work, us grave diggers think.
The language of empty space is very hard to speak.
Who standing at the open grave can help but believe?
A god crouched on his knees measuring the lives
born of woman must be one with a sense of humor.
What if after this life the next is the same?
Organs stuffed in jars wouldn't want saving.
Even the mummies ravel, I've been told,
their petrified bodies worn by air.

Though I evacuate the hole, the dignity of lowering
doesn't fall to my strong hands.
My tasks require no fancy clothes.
These days I use machines in digging.
Still sweat and shovels are my friends.
If I had a son I'd teach him early
the ground is for planting men,
to tend the garden under the moon
and leave the lies of headstones for fools.

To Give Something

I lounge in a stack of slick tires,
my arms dangling over the sides,
with wind quivering the rain
caught in a shriveled casing.
Broken springs rust in the sun,
dirty wads of cotton bloom
from the torn upholstery.

But I'm not here to complain
to all these bent bumpers
of the work I've left undone,
nor to celebrate the snaggled grilles.
But to give something—If only to stay
with my friend as he stands there,
his hand at his pants,
drenching the sour mud.

And into the weeds, into
the collapsed exhaust pipes
and the grease-caked engines
I throw the only thing I have:
An empty can.

Circles That Cost

I am the stranger
pushing through the aisle
where a boy wearing a white apron
marks in perfect circles
the cost of our lives.
I watch him triggering
his staccato gun,
then pick a can to check the season
knowing the one deadly date.
A child who may call her dog
by its bark, who must know
the stars but not their names
hides her face in the joy
of her hands and peeps
at me with her slyest grin.
But by now the cart is bulging
full as a belly
and first night is fastening on.
I shift a bottle
before it breaks, move
the eggs to the top of the basket
and head for the line
where the girl's smile
will make the price worth paying.

For One Who Has No Heart

This is the heart I bring
toward the top of the hill
in the still, grave silence.
This is the fist in my chest
clenching and unclenching.
This redneck heart that never
wants to learn, but takes pride
in working all night long,
he's the one I owe my life to,
this most remarkable heart
who's got no heart at all.

The Distance

The Distance

That night we walked in the Georgia dark
dogs barked and ran in circles.
Guided not by the star of Bethlehem
but by the beneficent sign of Texaco
we traveled toward the only light we saw.
Weariness grew in your arms as the child
began to cry. You opened your blouse
and filled the dark of his mouth.

When we were young, before we knew
the need of gasoline and failure,
years before we knew each other,
each of us had some vague expectation.
You believed in a man of great ambition,
a man of silence who only spoke
to give perfect commands. I predicted
a woman of alluring mystery
stepping from the quagmire of the future
like Venus on her moving shell.

But on that Georgia night we walked
the present was corporeal as the baby you held,
yet we were also our past and future.
For all we knew along the road
we walked may have been the last
resort of some distant generations
who would surely feel no resentment
we chose unknowingly to walk upon their
remembered bones; for when only
memory, doesn't existence end? Or
do we walk this road, always approaching,
the child forever at the breast, the mother

humming, the father measuring the distance
between this spot and the glowing next?

Arthritis

Sunday morning lies
with its light
in the streets,
the leaves swept
along the broken curb
and a bird burning
from its nest
with the first sun.

As the old man arises
moaning into shadows
and draws his life
into a long shiver
he thinks of a rabbit,
a fringe of white
blooming on the tail
that waves in the wind.

But he draws back
into the garden
of morning
and gathers his face
a withered flower
into the dawn.

If The Bacon Takes Time

If the bacon takes time
to wink at the egg
does that mean it knows
sulphur from gold?

When the baking potato whistles in the pan
its eyes wide from the grave
does the oven say, "Your body
is given for this hungry man"?

From the mound of salt sprinkled
in the palm, can a measure be changed
to sugar? Can the lamb
decline to be mutton?

When the right hand holds
the fork, the left takes up the bread.
If the hollow of mouth
is filled by food

the lips that are fish
have already fed,
the snake of a tongue
has slithered.

Once a woman woke and opened
her eyes on the dark,
and remembered only then
that she was blind.

But she found her way
to the kitchen, and holding

her hand over the flame
began the ritual of cooking.

Trappings

She sits by a table, where an imaginary
Plumbline could follow her spine and lower legs.
She is wearing heels with see-through toes.
A delicate cup and saucer are by her elbow.
A ship sails in the background mural.
On the bank consisting of boulders
Are gentlemen, and ladies with parasols.
The top of the table with cabriole legs
Shines so that it reflects
The perfectly polished samovar.
Earrings match her eyes and are
As delicate as her bones. A half smile
Is mysteriously on her lips, through which
Show eight deliciously white teeth.
Hair that could only be described
As flowing tresses and lips
That extend to perpendiculars
Dropped from the centers of her eyes
Are prominent features.
Her heavy French gown is silver, or perhaps
Gold; the picture is in halftone.
A buffet at her right background
Matches the dark mahogany table.
A floral continues along the wall.
Her sex is classically apparent
In the casual exactness of the folds
Of her gown. The picture
Is pointedly commercial, but on
An elegant scale. Men will buy
Not the fragrance she's selling,
But of course herself.
Women who view the photograph

Will not study it intently,
Though they will read the bold caption,
And many will be trapped.

The Carter House in Franklin, Tennessee

We go into the house
where the five generals had lain
in a blood smeared row,
their uniforms torn. Their bodies
small, still, and gray.
We see their medals do not shine,
and the battle flag furls, limp
on its splintered staff.

Under this floor we hear of the iron casket
bearing a glass window. In it would
be buried the youngest general,
whose face, when he's raised a century later
by robbers looking for Confederate gold,
would be so well preserved with arsenic
the marauders would throw down
their shovels and run, believing
they'd uncovered the haunted dead.

Somewhere in the house they laid
the Carter's eldest son, returning
from his soldier's duty.
Not five hundred yards from his own
front porch he fell from Union fire
and bled to death before his friends
could carry him to his nearby home,
where bloodless he was laid
upon the quilted bed.

Into his same house slaves had brought
pork and veal, greens and pickled eggs.
As they came from kitchen, entering

the breezeway, marching toward the dining
room, each one was made to whistle,
for fear they'd steal the master's bread.
In line, we ask about the portraits:
stern faces, on bodies not their own.
We're shown the swinging shelves
used to confound the mice and rats,
told in little rooms the children slept.

Benediction in Memphis

In this "City of Good Abode"
where God smiles from his church
on every other corner
and Satan stands straight
as a spark plug
the preacher comes on in color
because his patrons have willed it.
But in this tavern the TV blurs.
Here I'm near my friend
who's five blocks back
under the mercy of nurses
where his body slowly fills
with the weight of death.
But this room reeks of lonely life,
and across the aisle
three bony rogues play with dice
for drinks and change.
One swears to a woman
he's bigger than any man
and from under the table
pulls forth a magic dildo
he says must prove it.
But the woman who's with his friend
says she's seen better—
Outside in the oil
that covers the street
and becomes night
I've got my Harley waiting.
And since the great saints
of all useless travels
do not forbid it,
I ride through the broad streets

thinking of my friend in his last hours,
and cursing this best
of all possible machines,
I hear in the last rites of wind,
in the benediction of engines, in
the confession of gears,
that every shaft
turns for something.

Saying It All

Sitting here with wings
that fold up into my shoulders,
before my eyes the three ways of light,
my fragile shirt unbuttoned
to take greedily of the breeze,
I await in this room
the long close of night.

Surrounded by half the hours
of my one full time, by a chest
of lions biting rings in their
mouths and an eagle on a mirror
skipping a rope of stars,
I step free for the moment.

Only to come back, past
this empty whiskey jug
that may have been
my father's father's,
but belonged only to clay
or to the heat that held
its hands over the glaze.

And once back, draining
the last night's drink,
I'm trying again.
Nothing so ambitious
as to loose the great knot
of fate, but to settle
for a few words that might sing
some needed grace.

So from a table, holding a lamp
living in its own light,
I take this open book
and move my fingers along the lines
trying to find a place.
Until a drift of words
mounds like flesh.

And I think of a mother's breasts
that must have sweetened to life
in my mouth. This mouth
that wants to live on words,
but must give back every one.
This mouth that opens
to say it all, and says all
by saying nothing.